Love Is In The Air

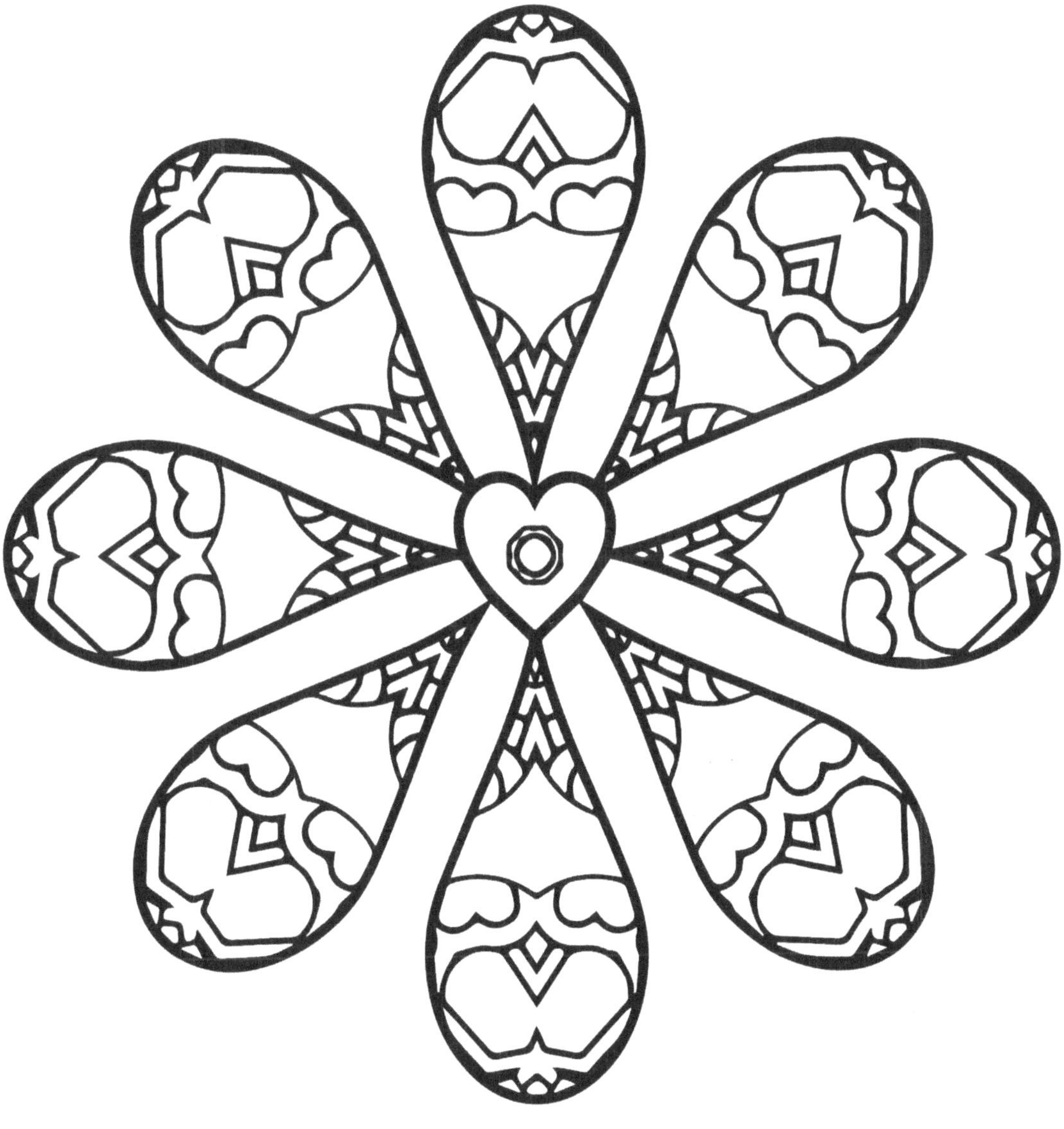

Coloring2Relax

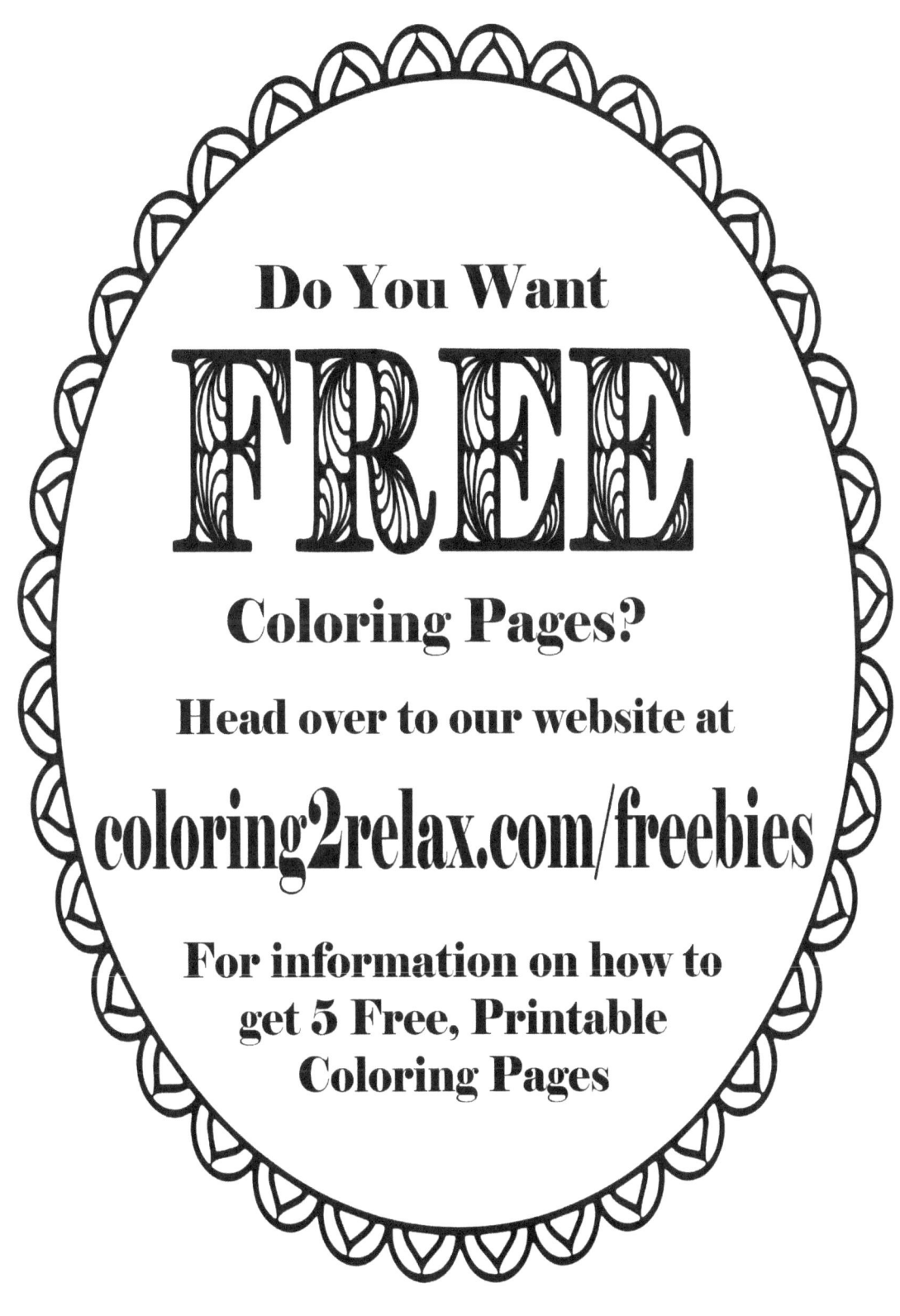

Do You Want

FREE

Coloring Pages?

Head over to our website at

coloring2relax.com/freebies

For information on how to
get 5 Free, Printable
Coloring Pages

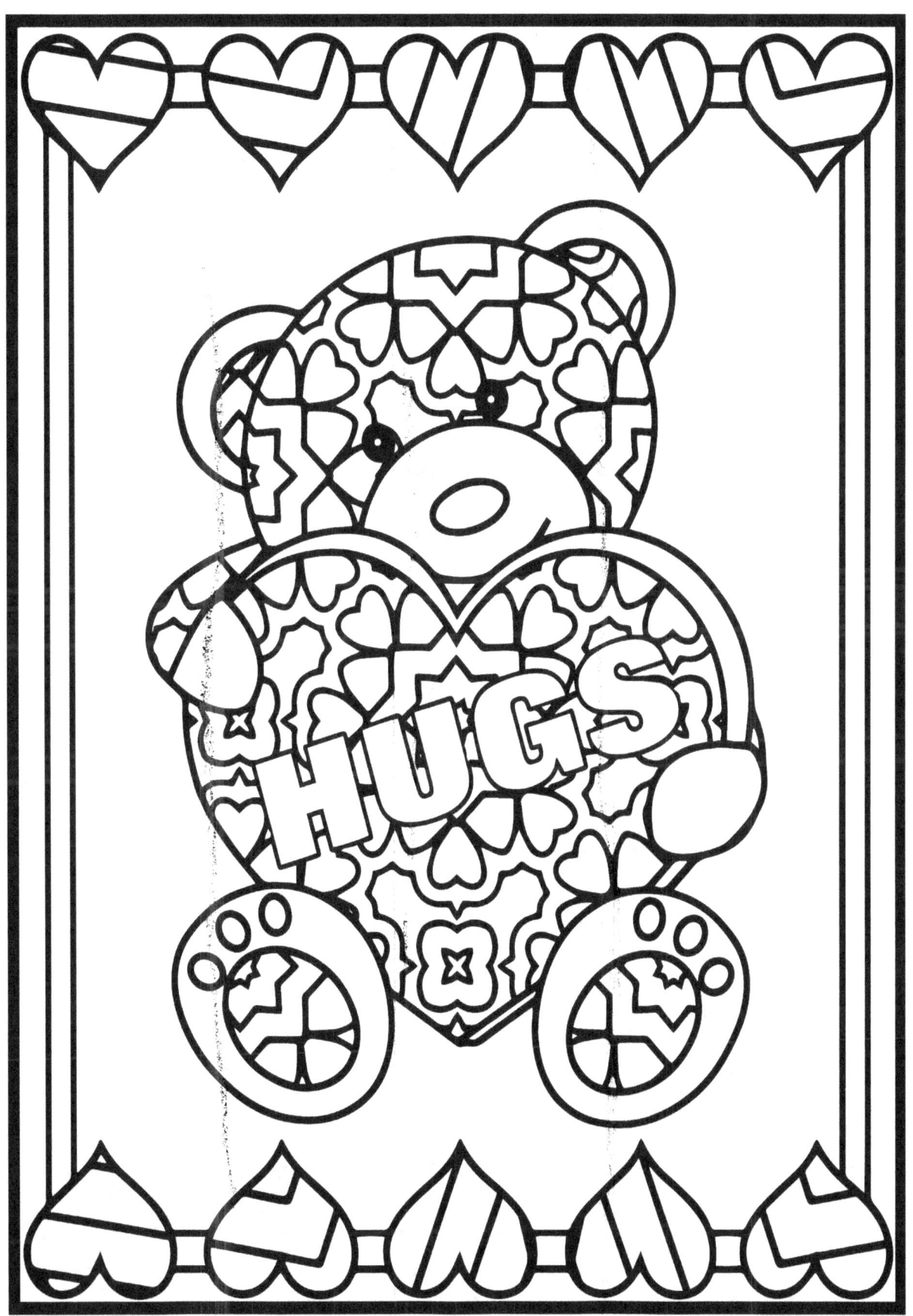

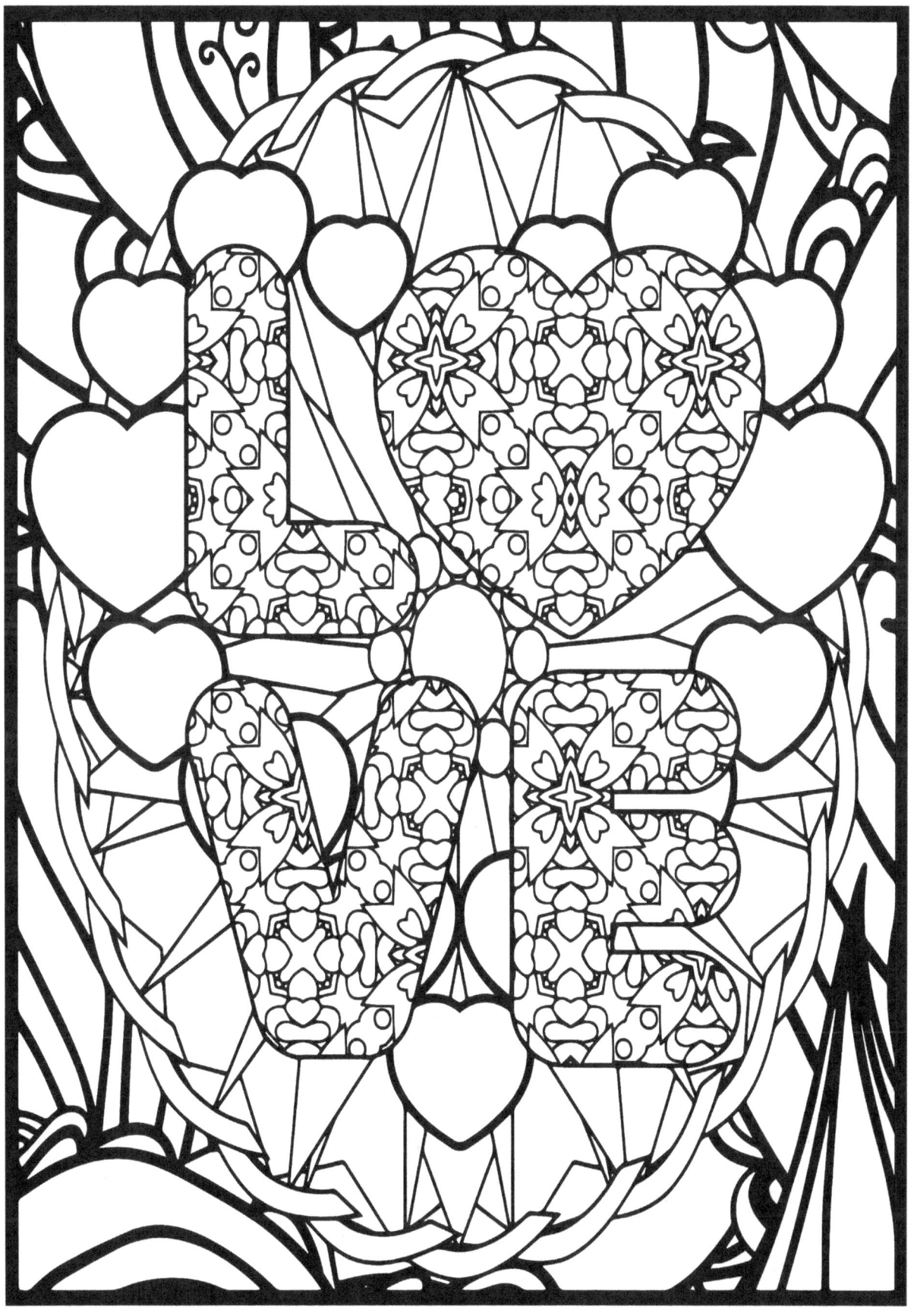

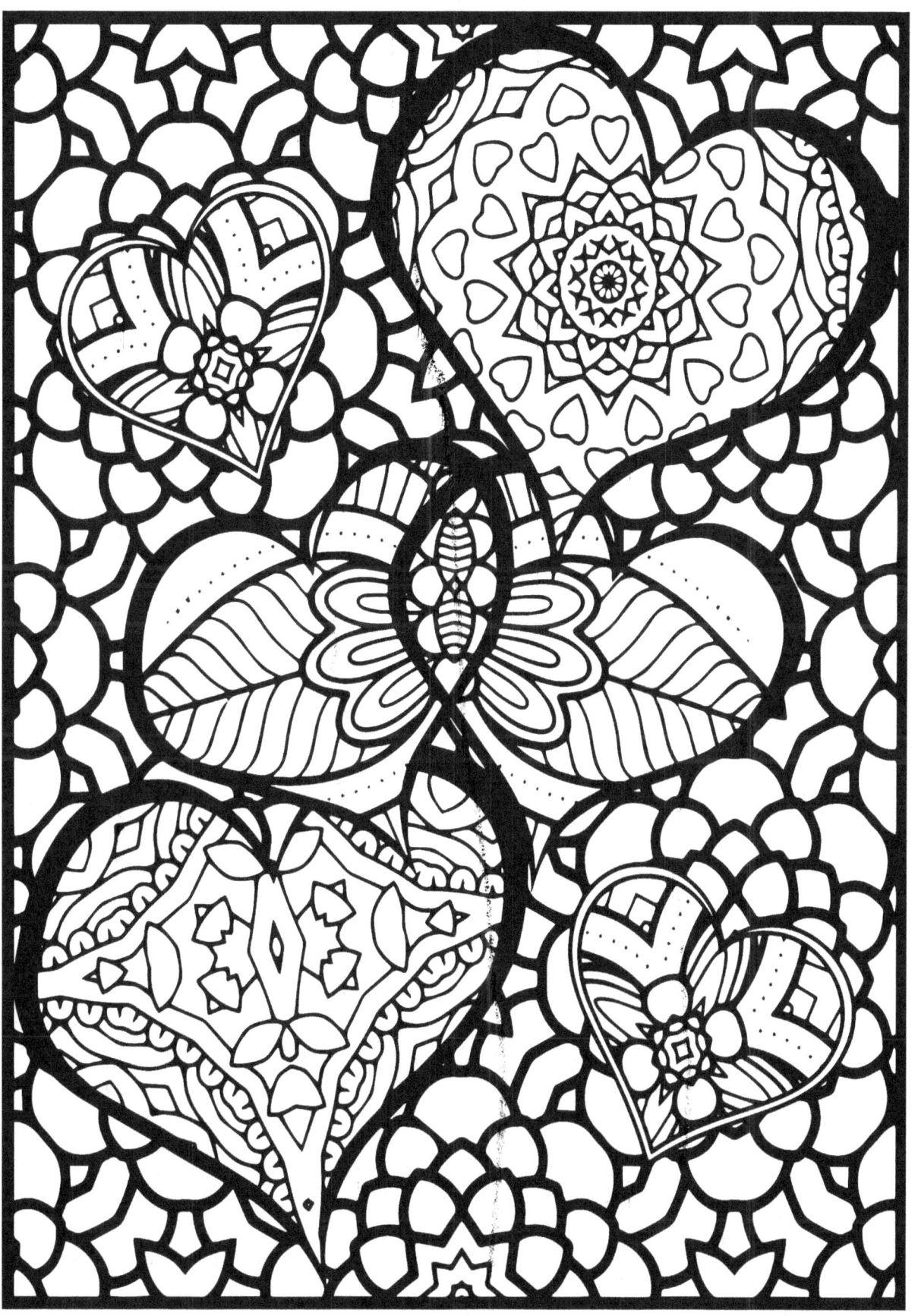

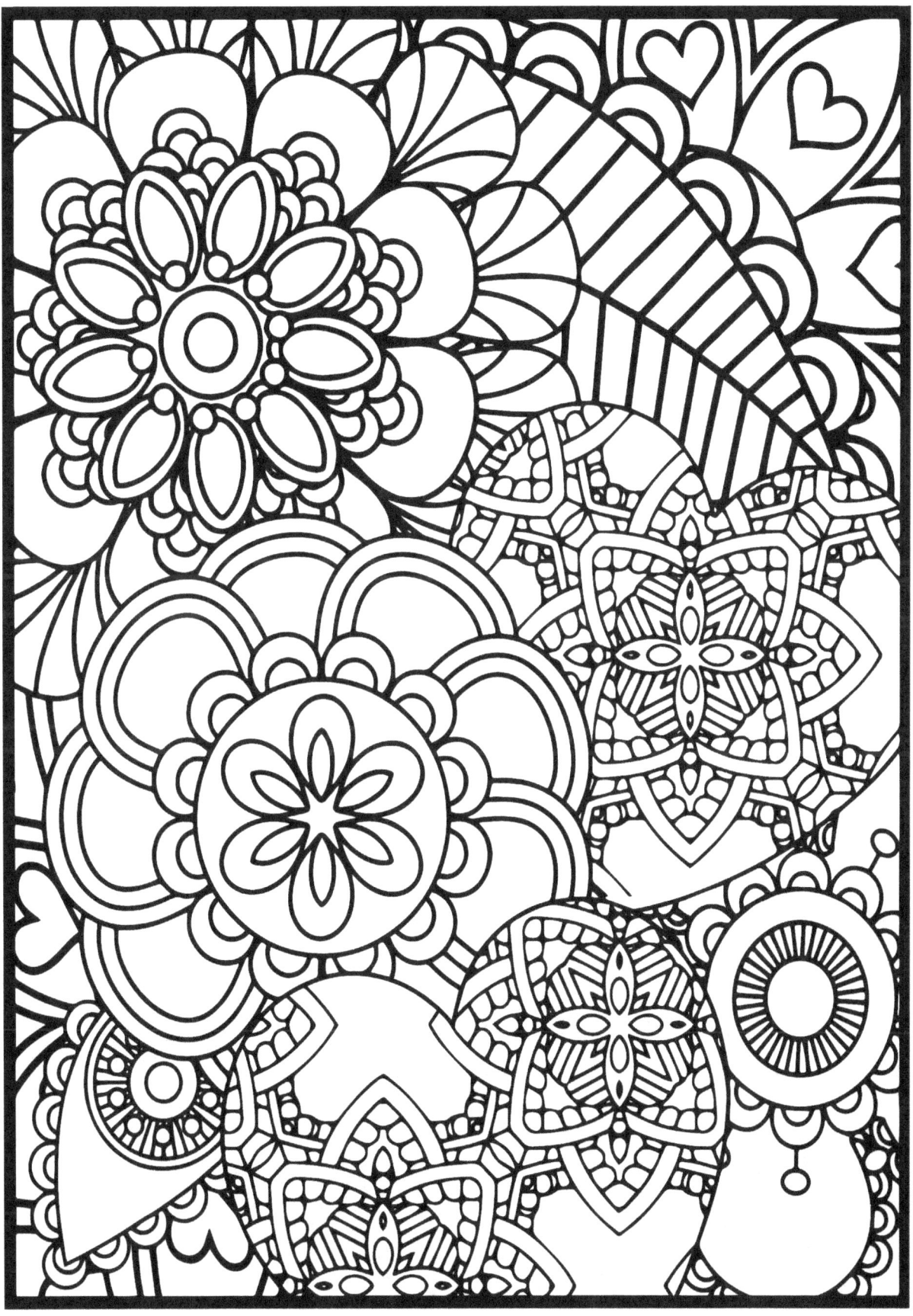

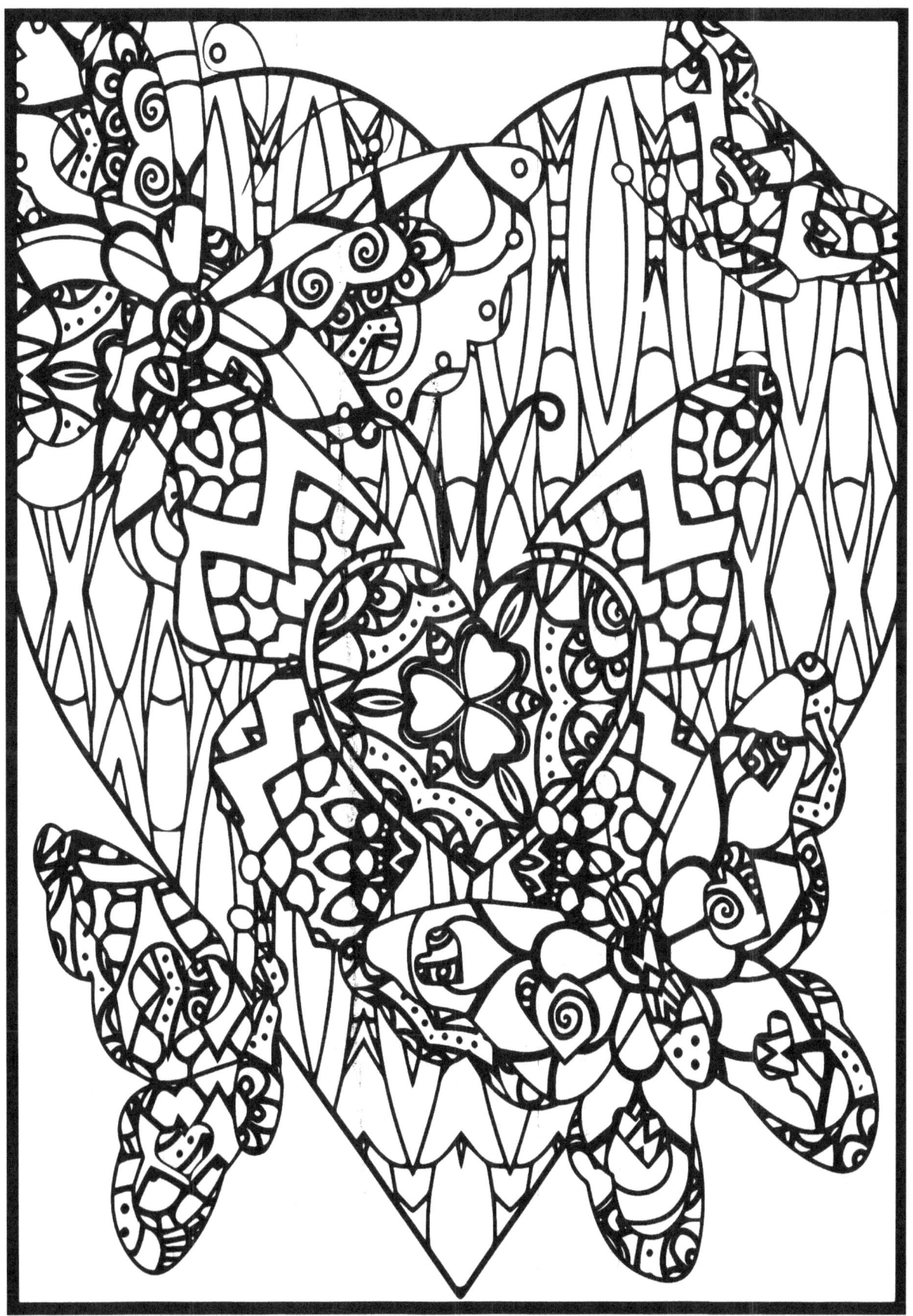

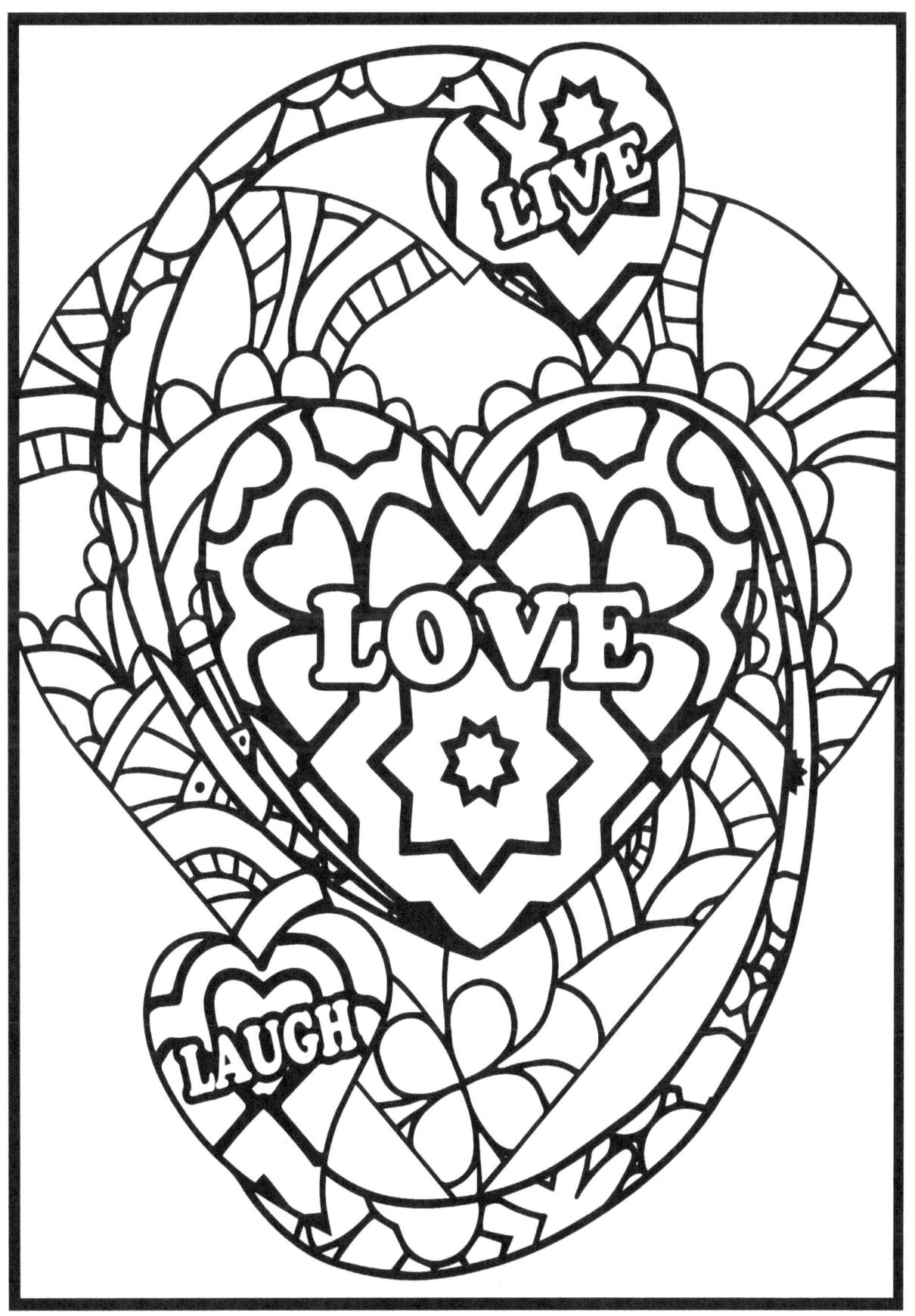

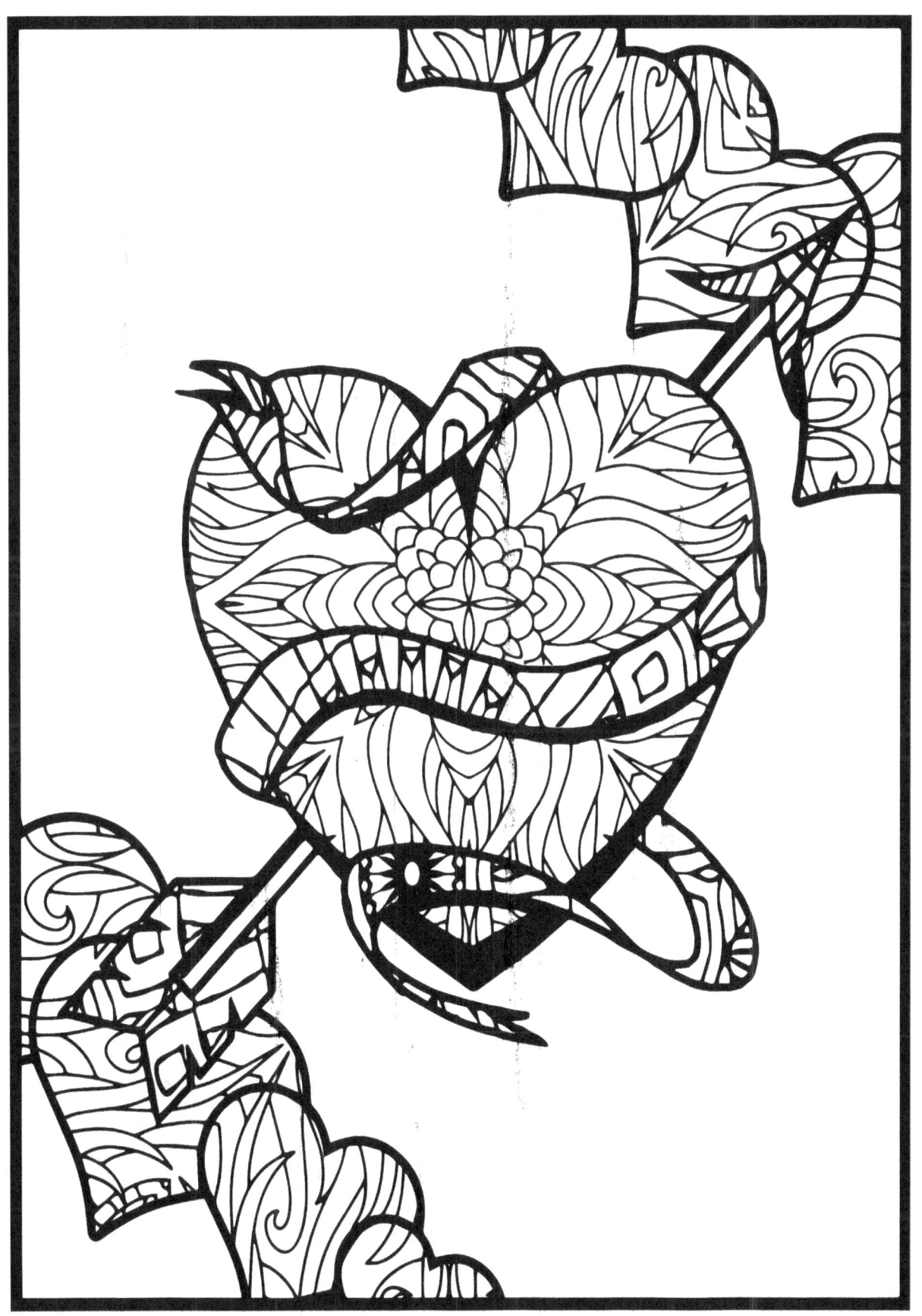

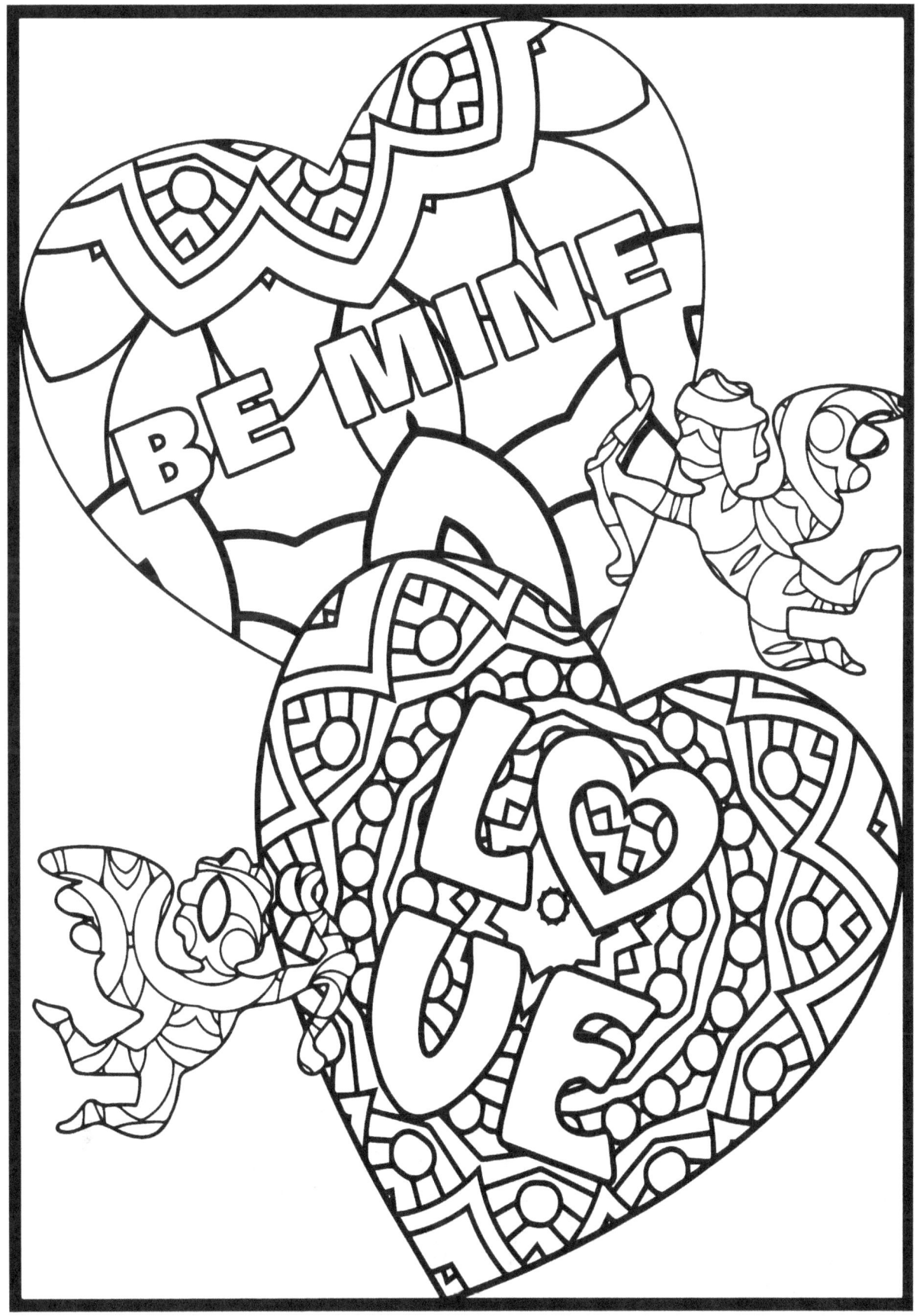

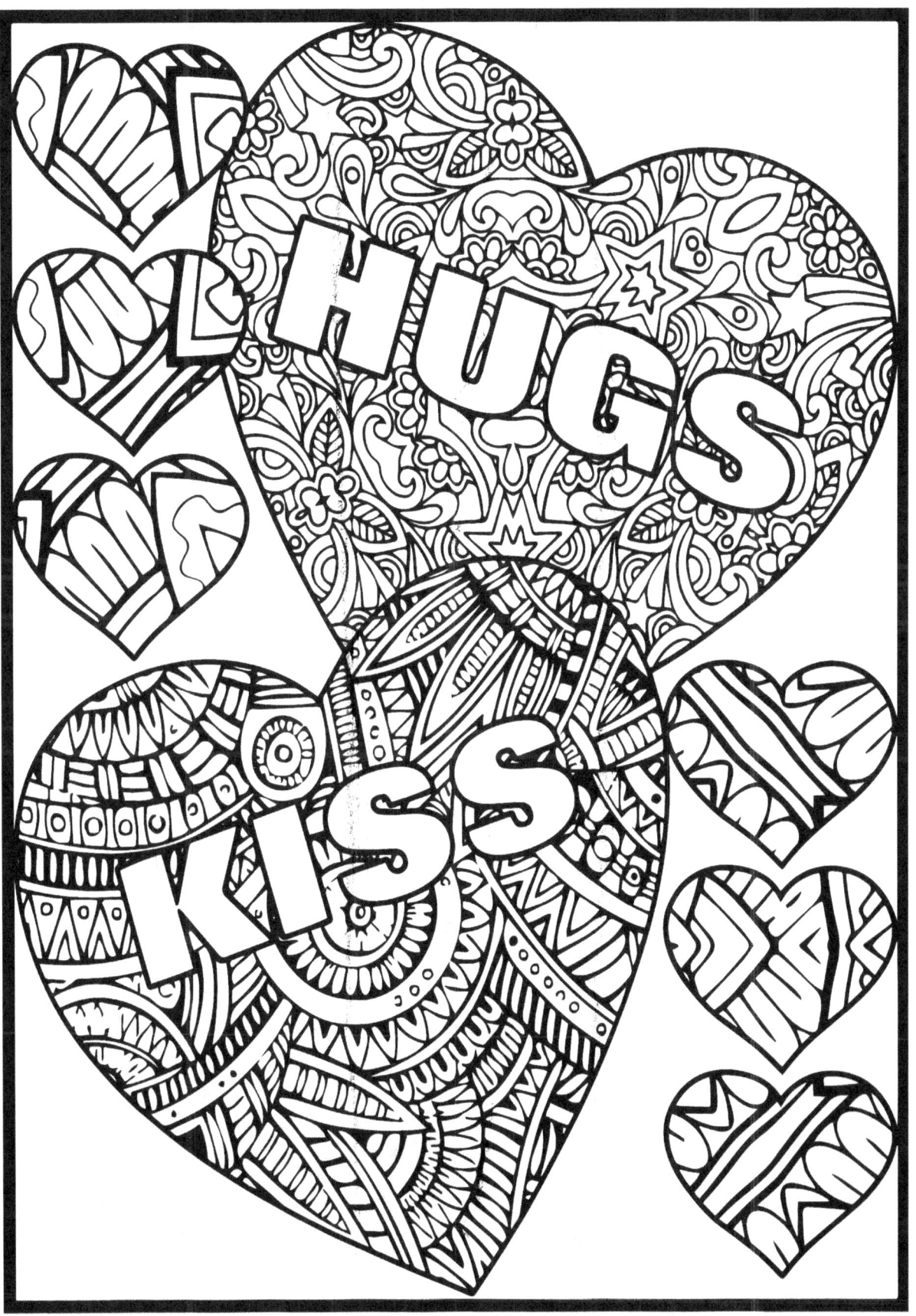

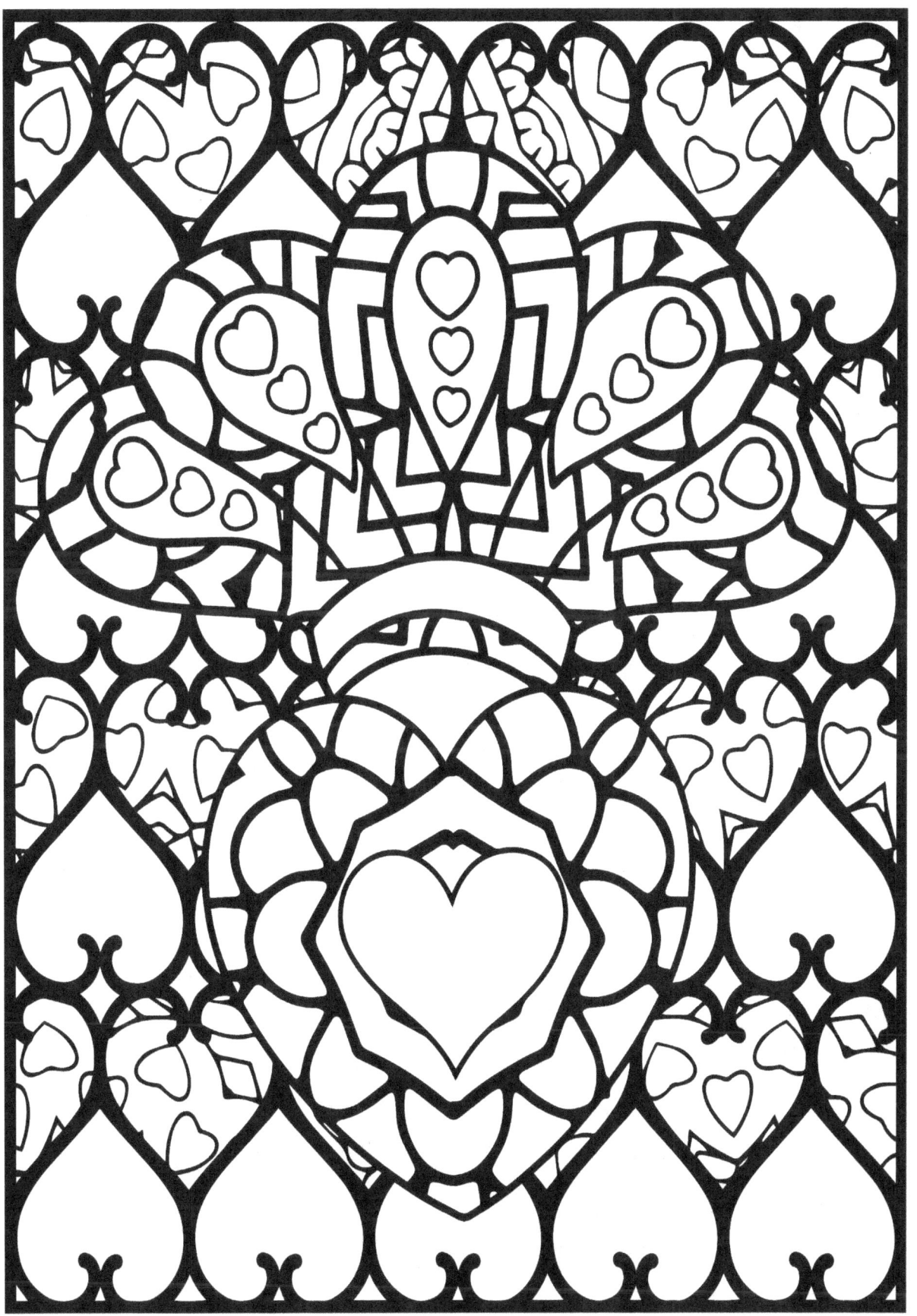

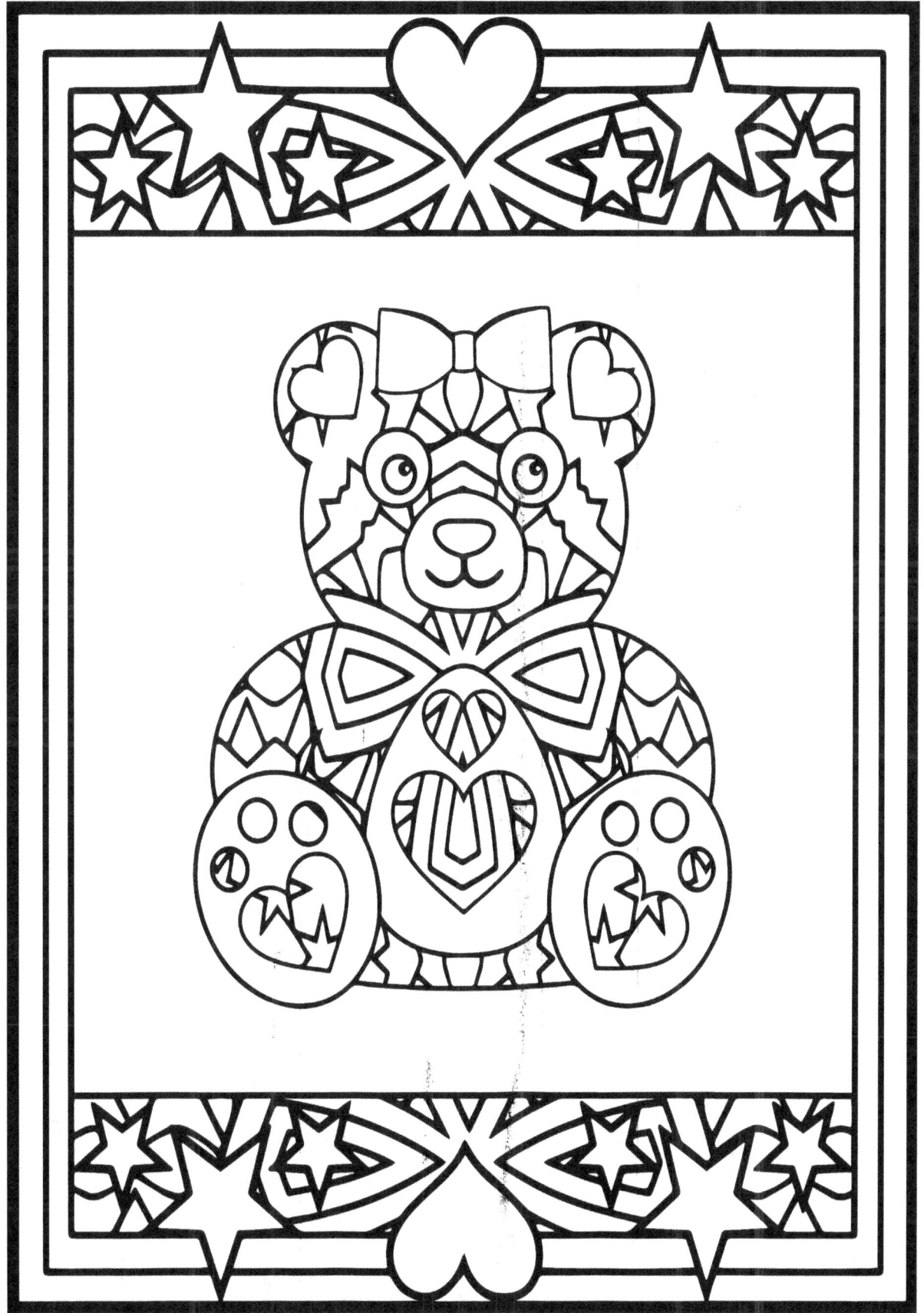

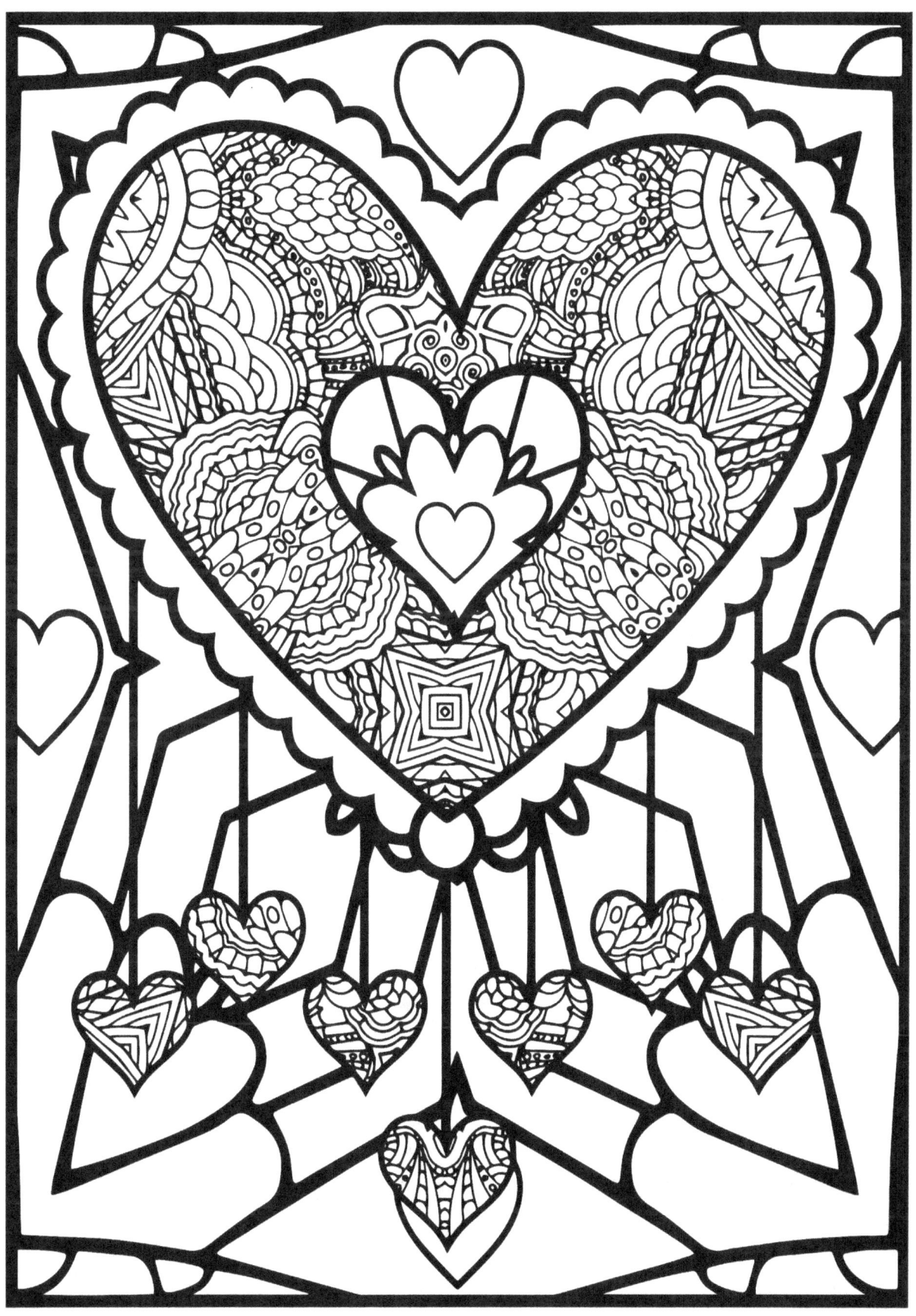

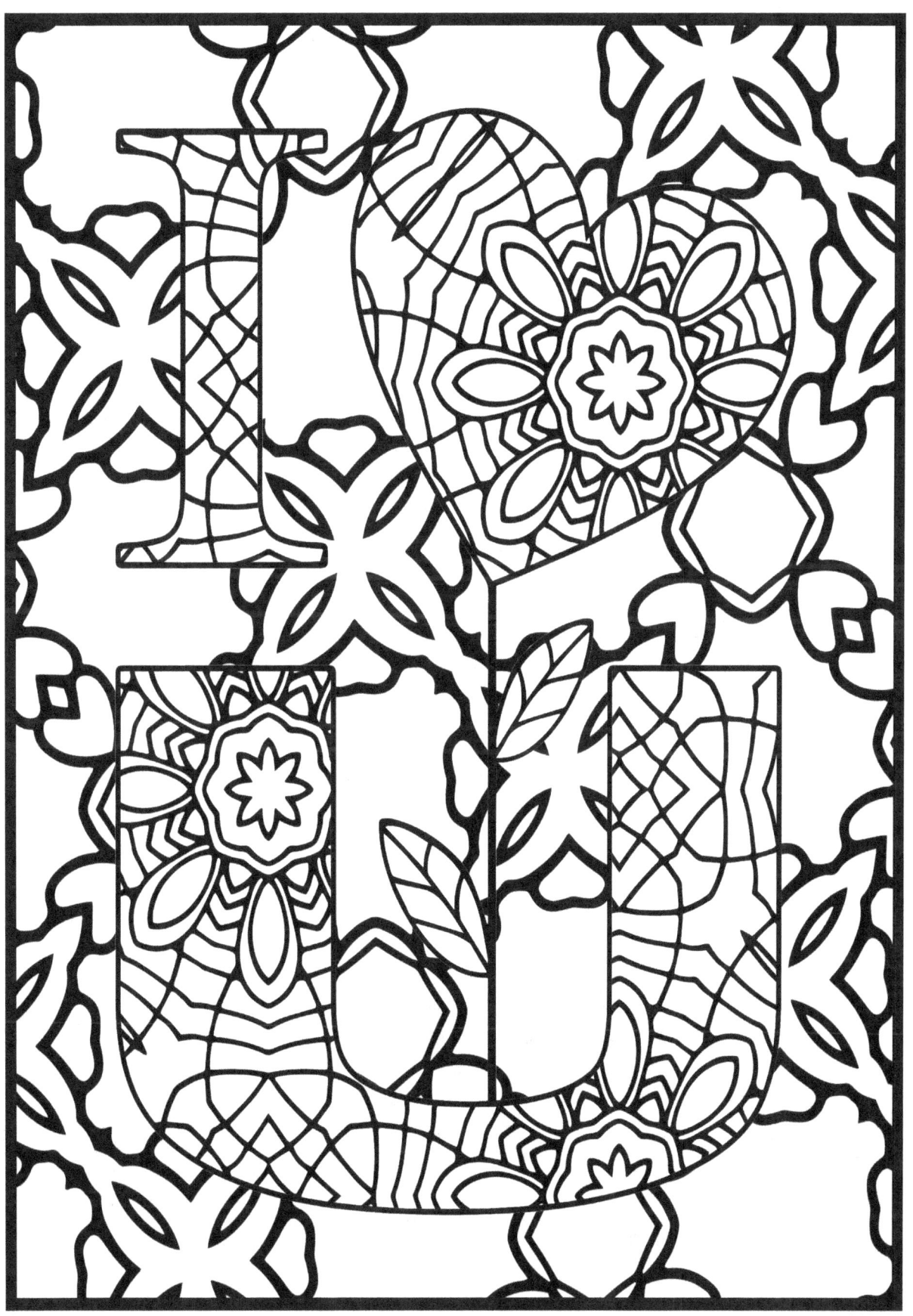

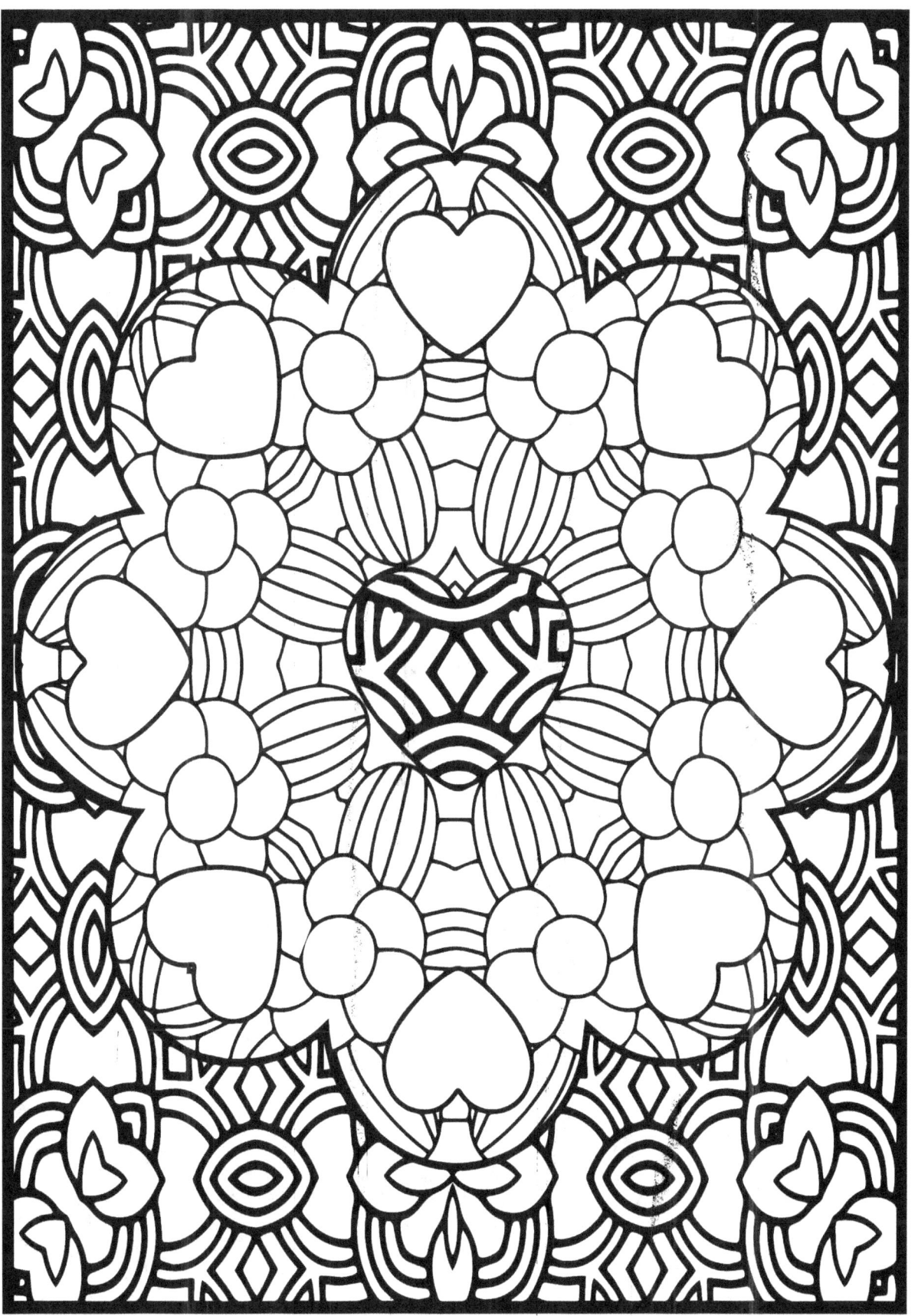

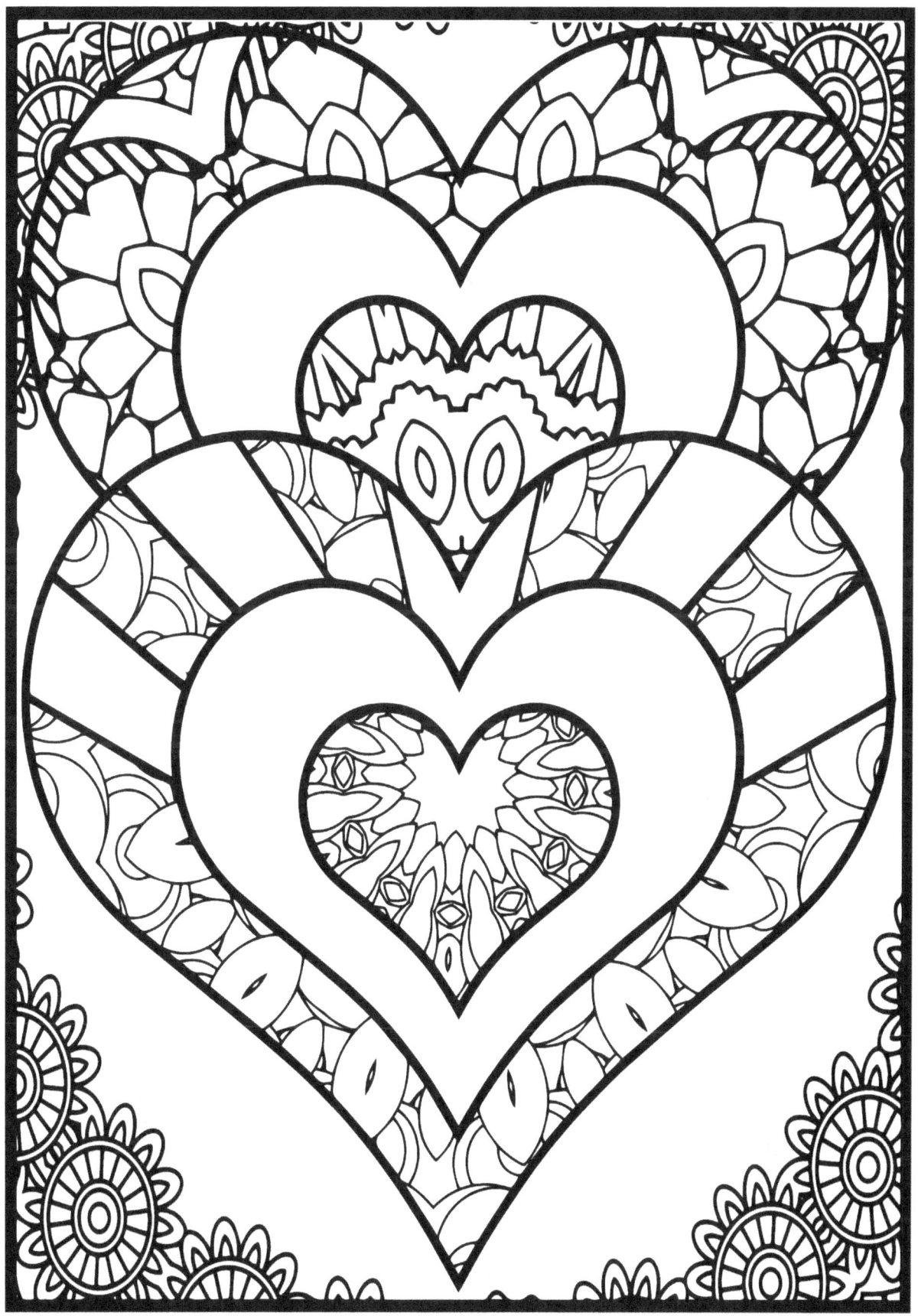

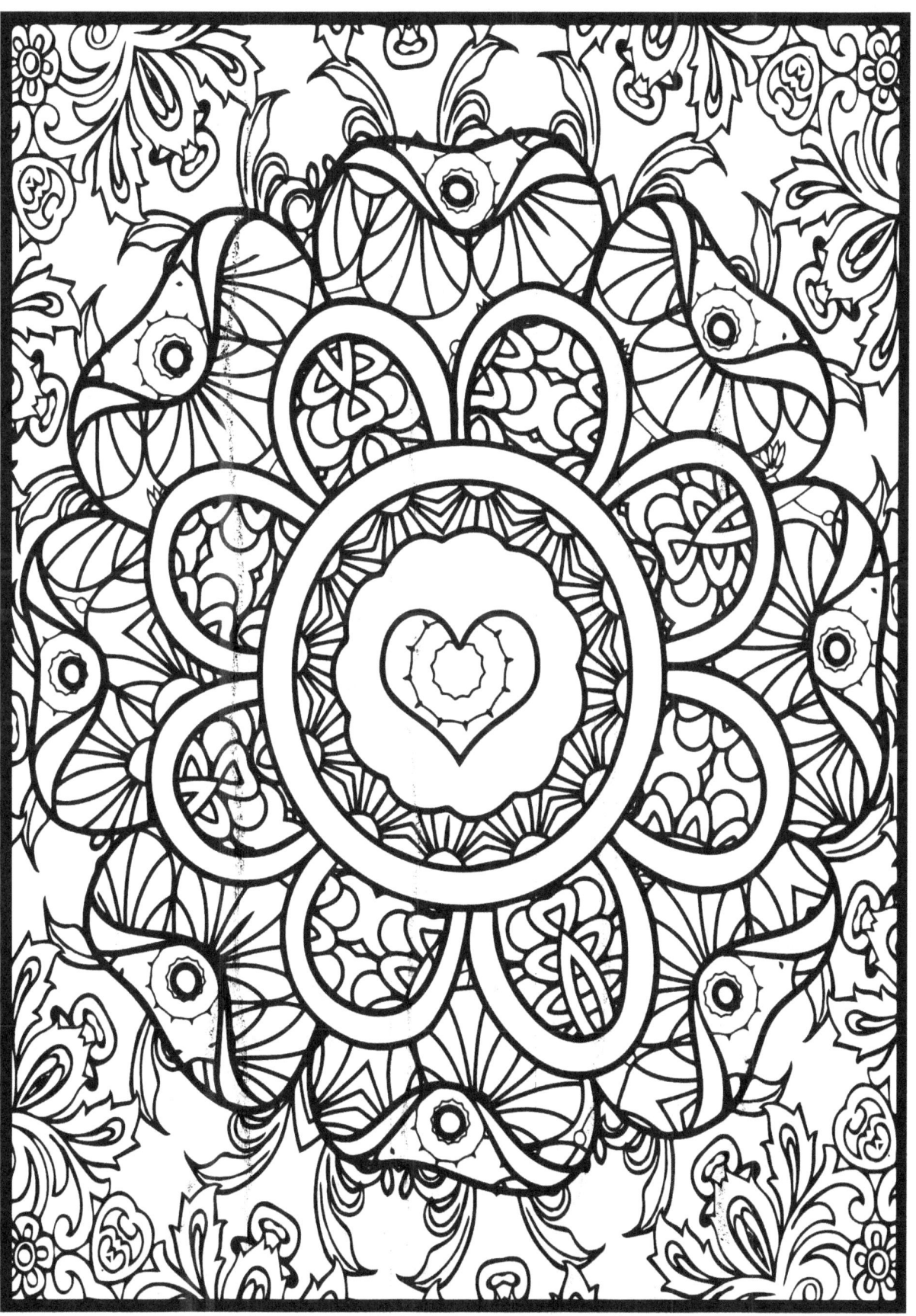

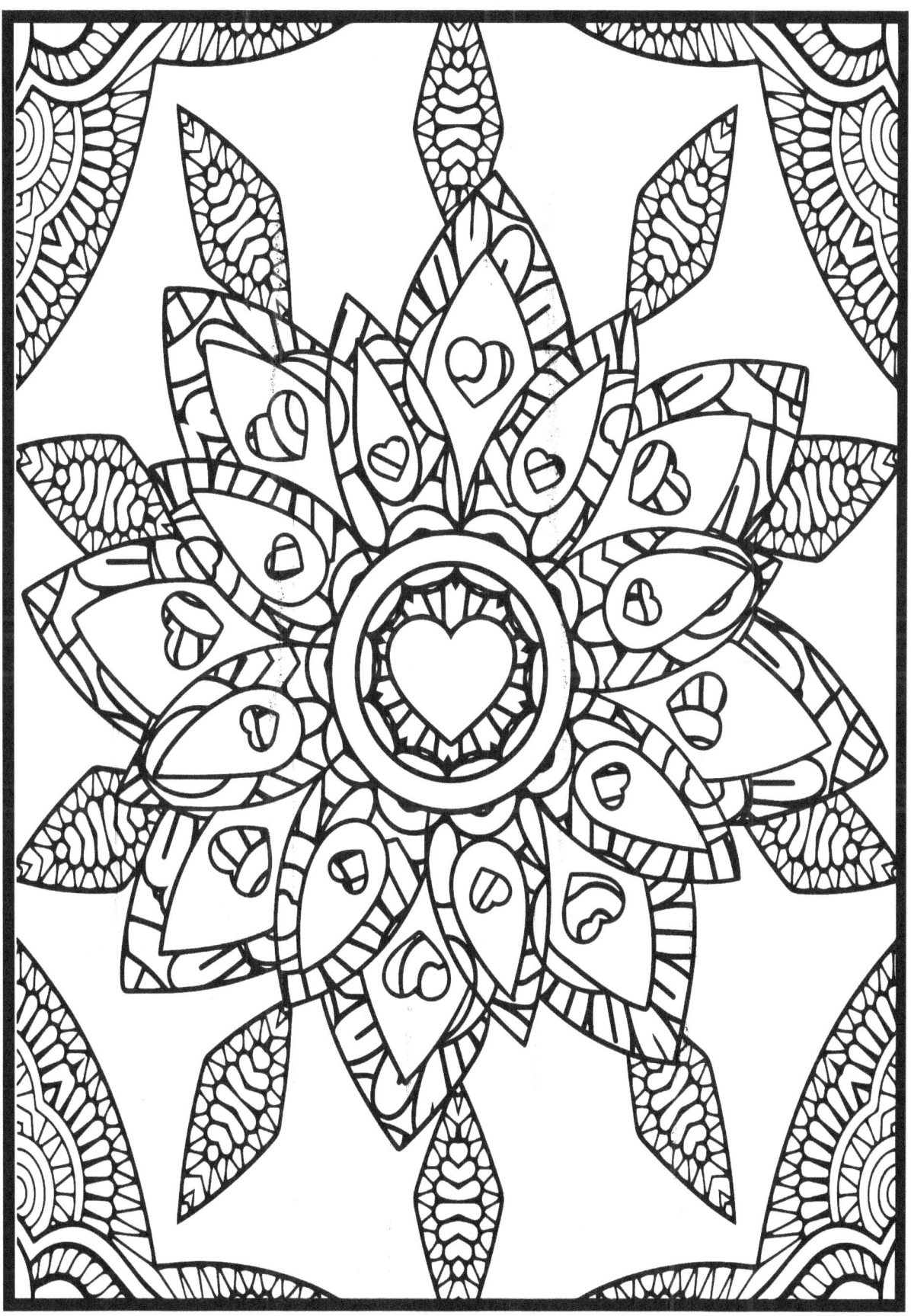

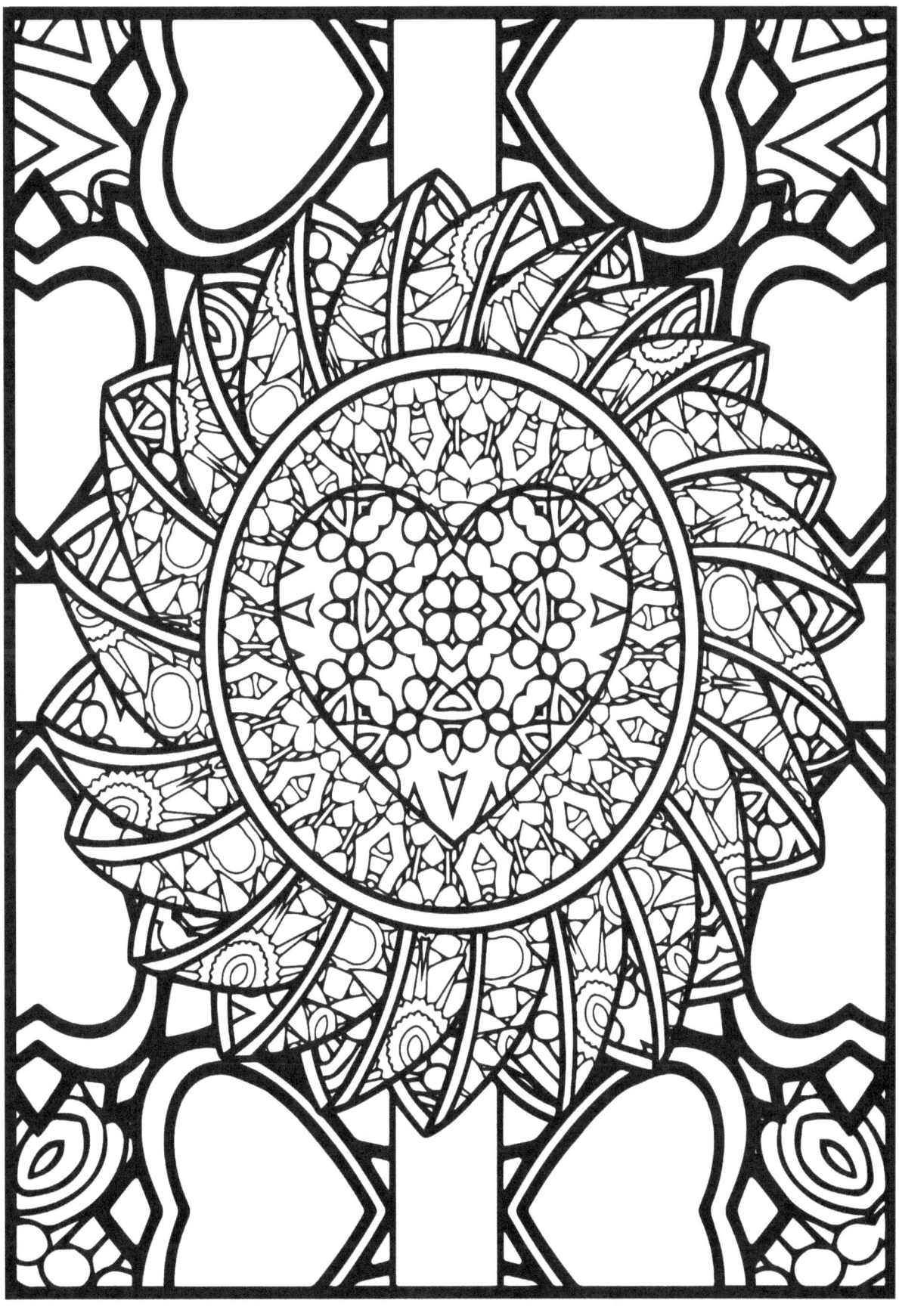

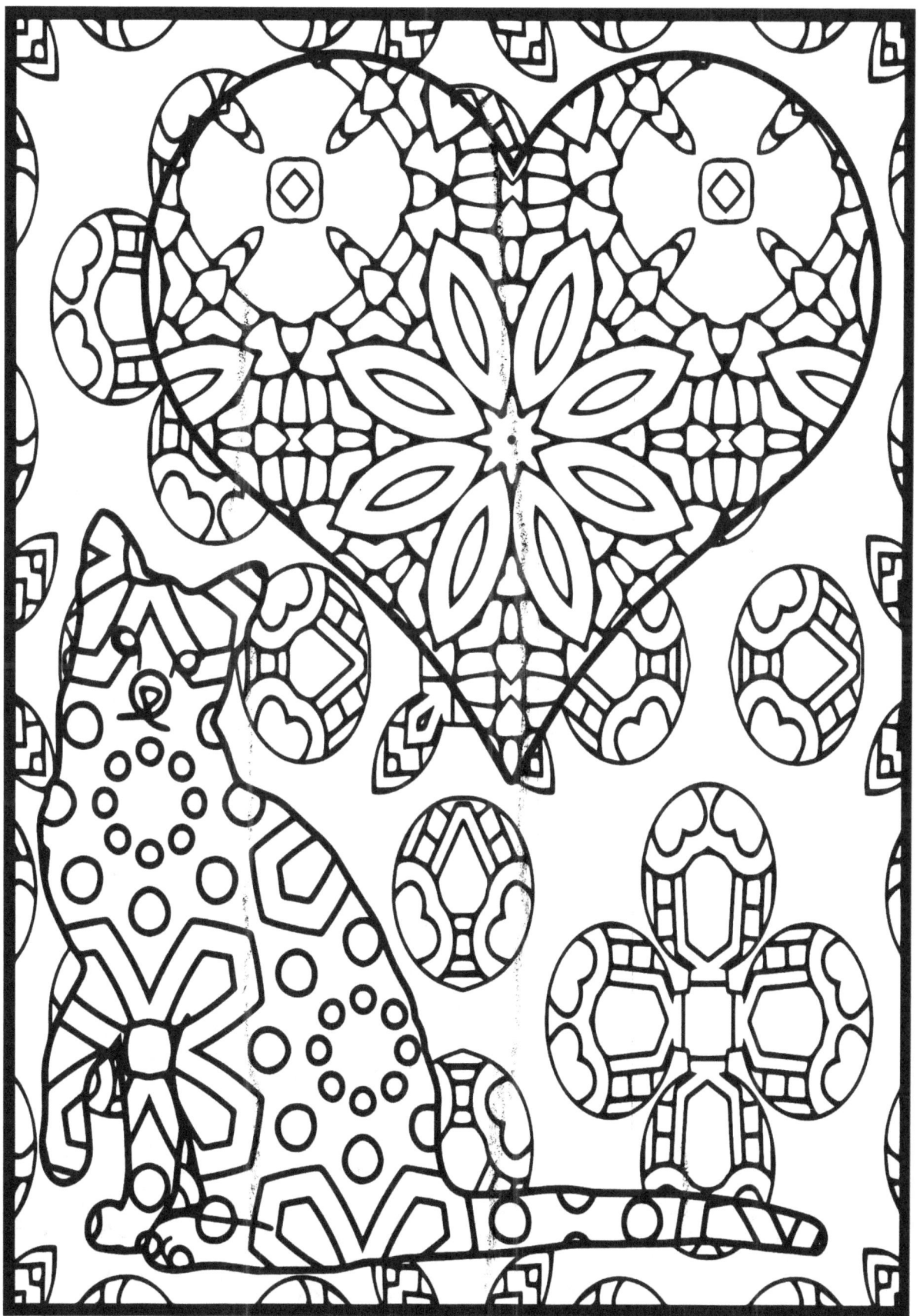

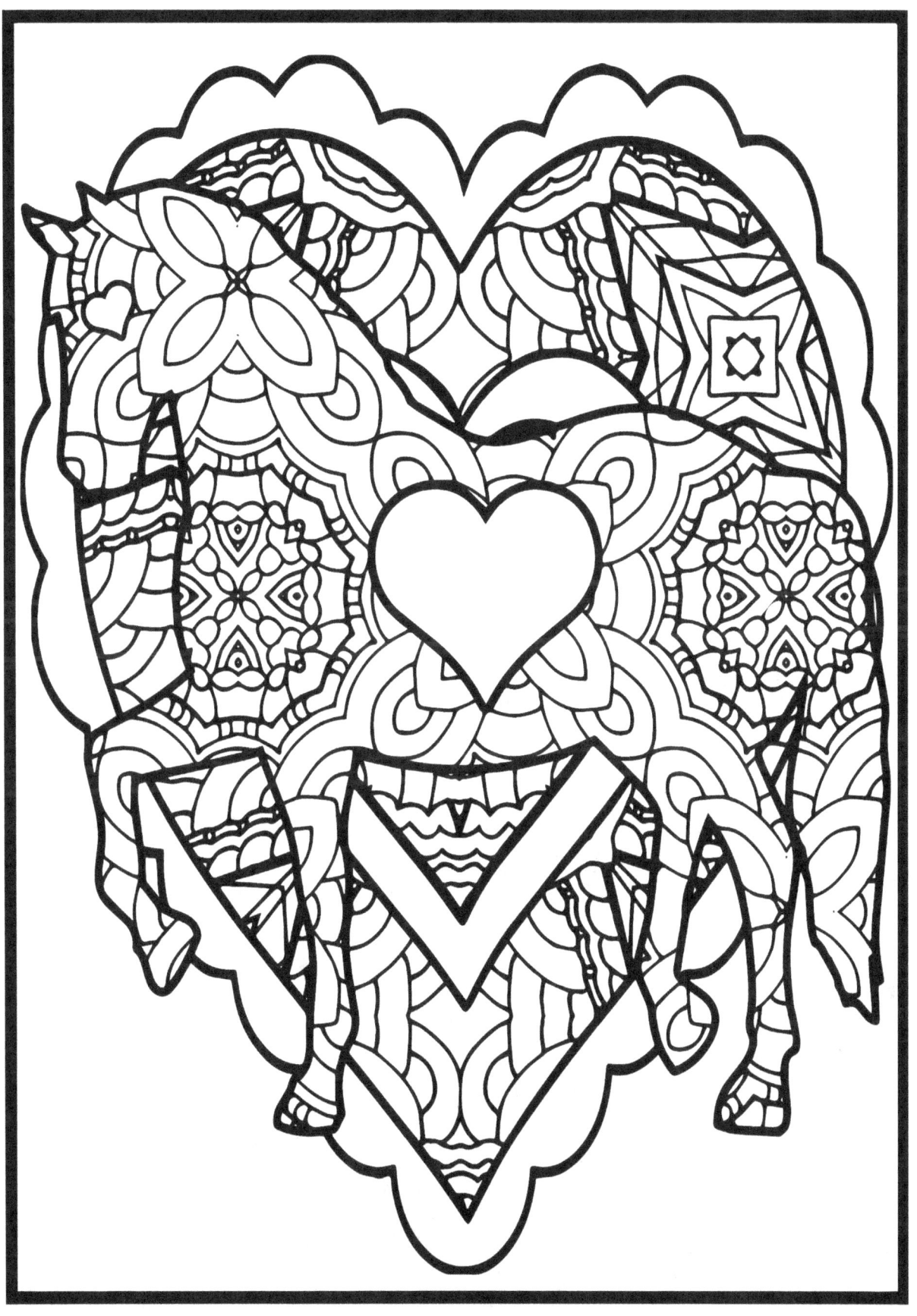

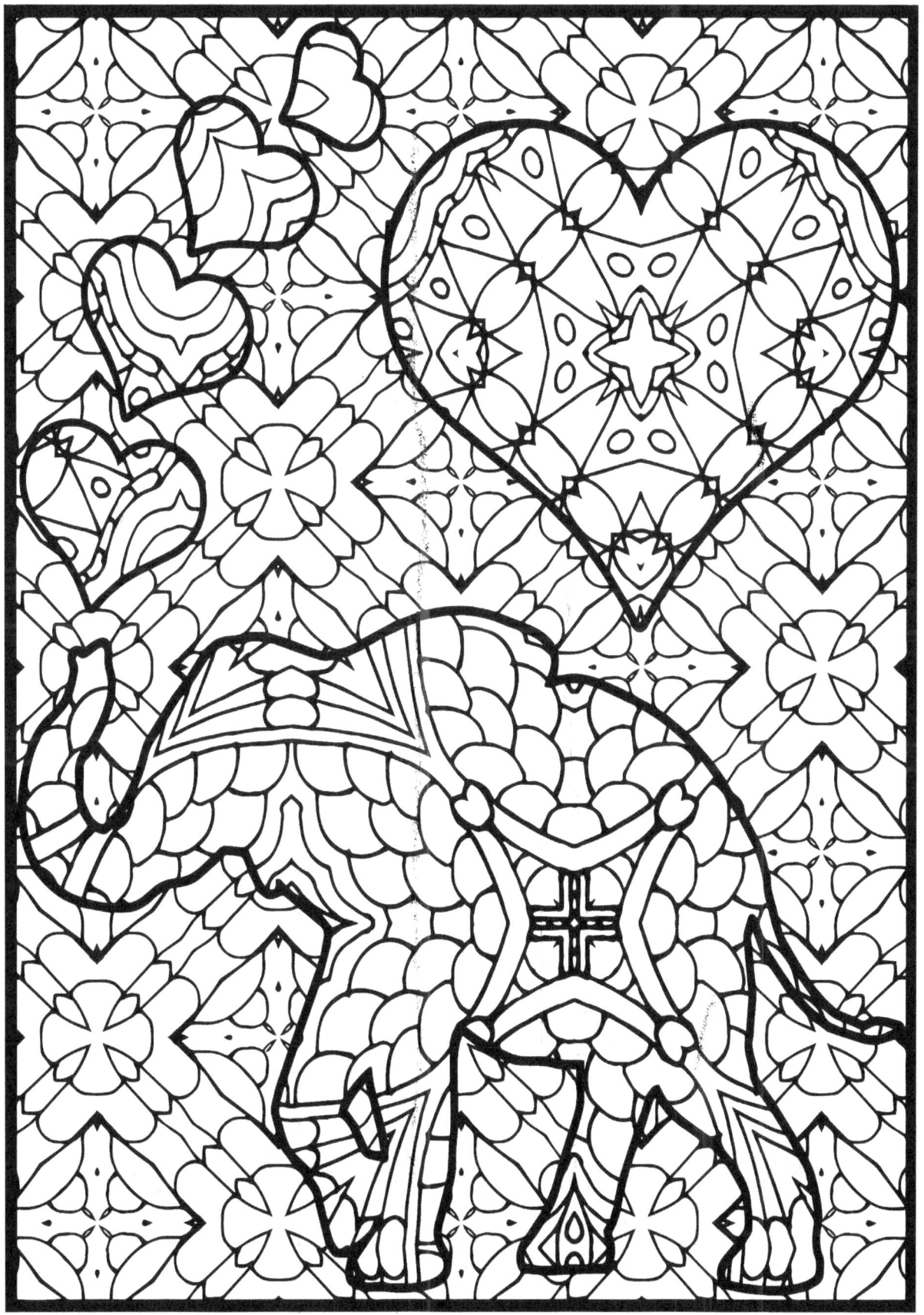

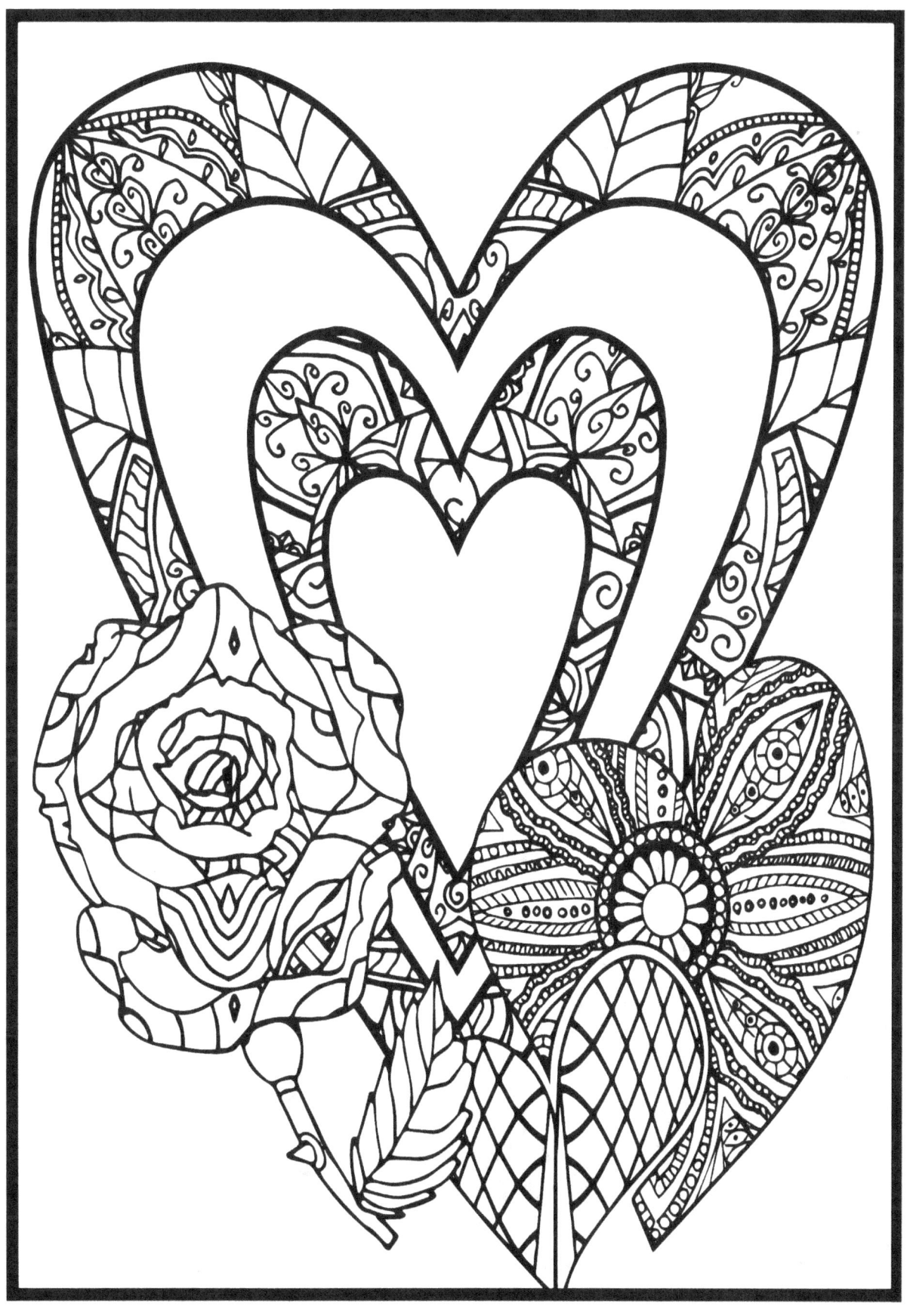

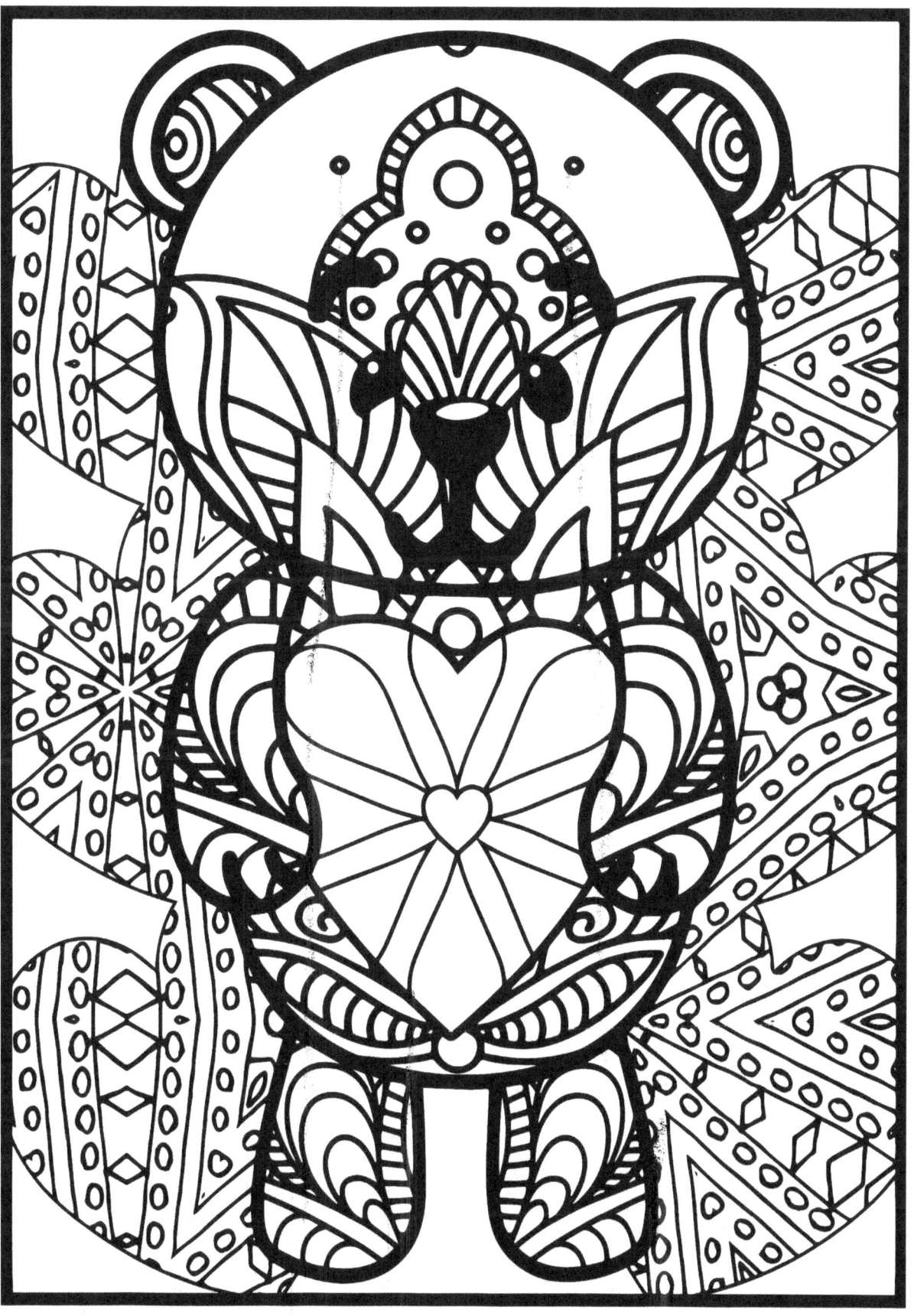

Coloring Practice Page

Practice blending & Shading, try new colors, test markers & gel pens,
decide on color palettes or add color palettes you want to use later

Coloring Practice Page

Practice blending & Shading, try new colors, test markers & gel pens,
decide on color palettes or add color palettes you want to use later

Coloring Practice Page

Practice blending & Shading, try new colors, test markers & gel pens,
decide on color palettes or add color palettes you want to use later

Coloring Practice Page

Practice blending & Shading, try new colors, test markers & gel pens,
decide on color palettes or add color palettes you want to use later

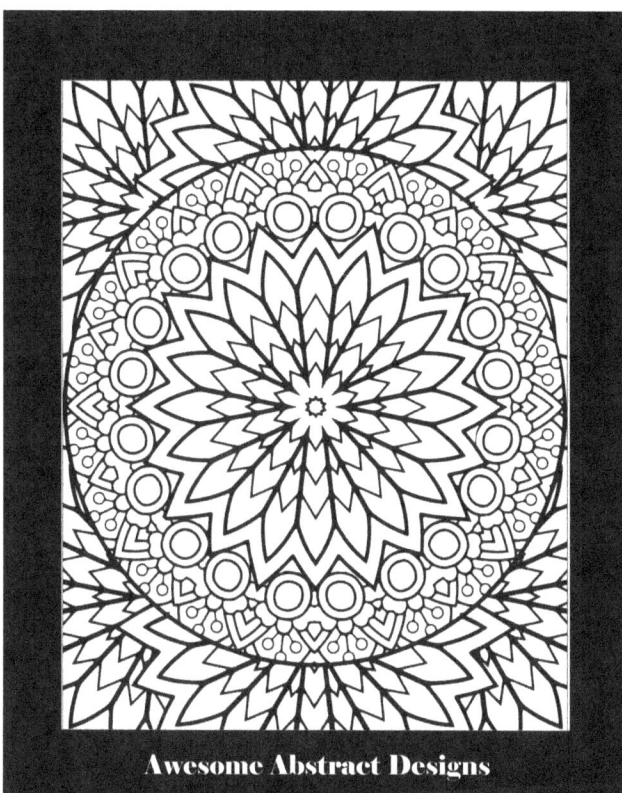

Awesome Abstract Designs

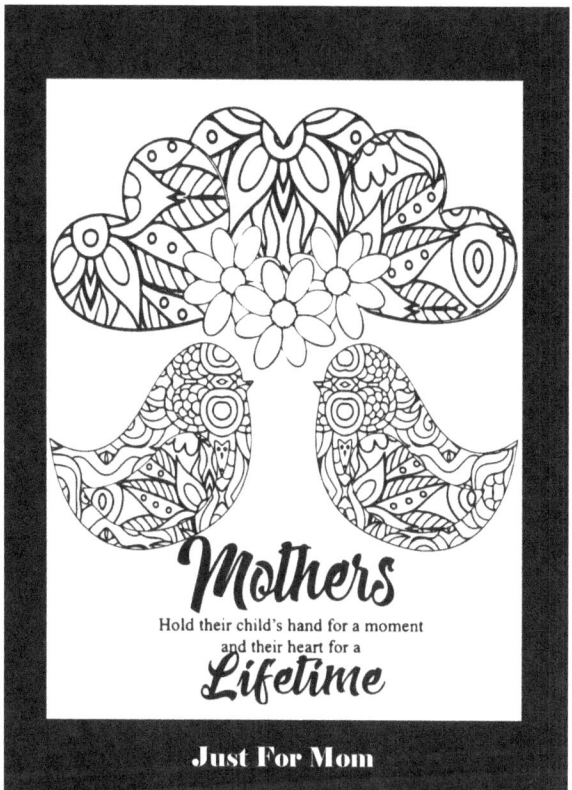

Mothers

Hold their child's hand for a moment
and their heart for a
Lifetime

Just For Mom

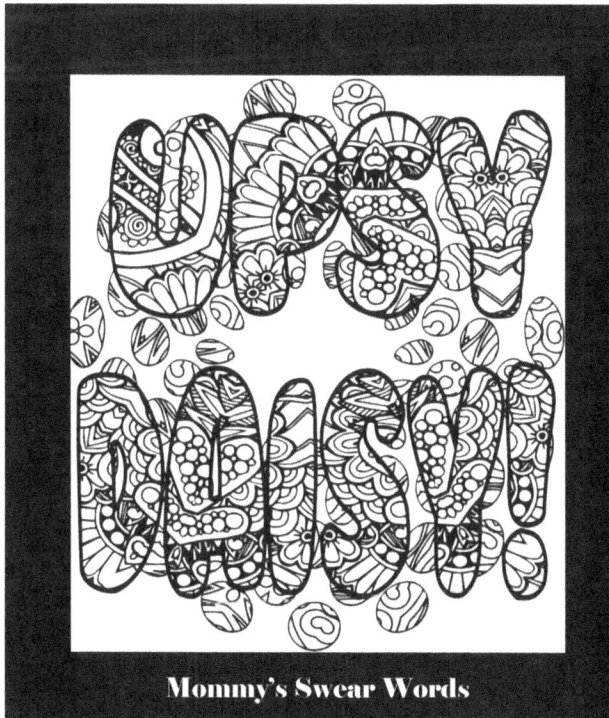

Mommy's Swear Words

Mommy's Swear Words, Midnight Edition

Remember to visit www.coloring2relax.com/freebies
for your FREE Printable Coloring Pages

Blank Page

Tear out and use under the page you are coloring for added protection against bleed through and denting

Blank Page

Tear out and use under the page you are coloring for added protection against bleed through and denting

Blank Page

Tear out and use under the page you are coloring for added protection against bleed through and denting

www.ingramcontent.com/pod-product-compliance
Lightning Source LLC
Chambersburg PA
CBHW081738170526
45167CB00009B/3863